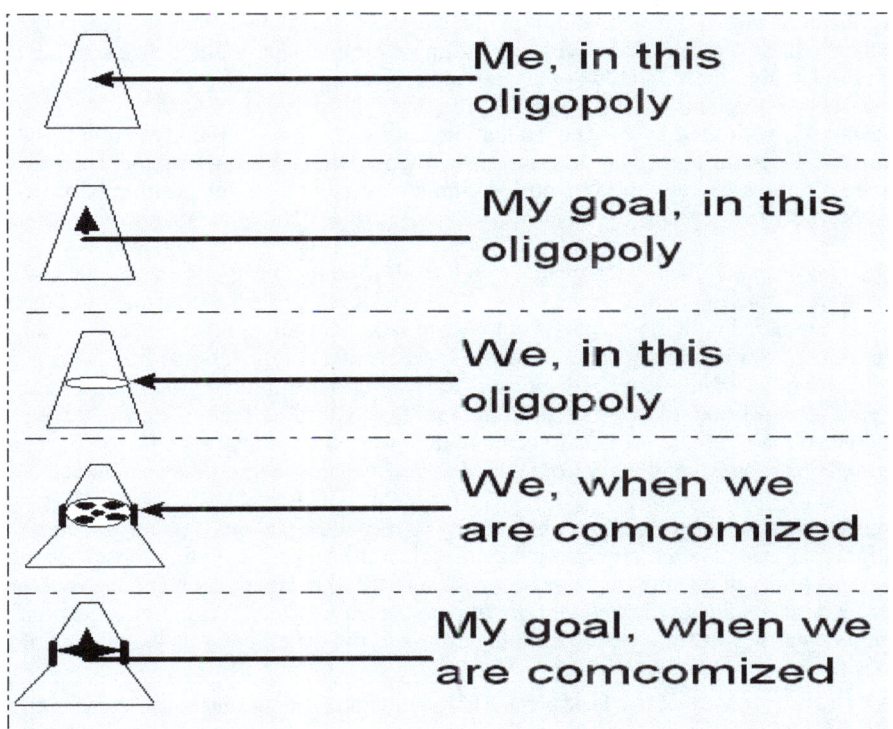

1. What it's about? *Putting the peers at the top of their unit!* ComComizing unit, or establishing a COMmon COMpany, is about individual ownership over the properties of that unit. Some (if not all) such owners are its "peer owners" having equal share of ownership over one portion of the unit, as all the other owners (if any) are its "ordinary owners".

The distribution of such individual ownership is defined in a short personal agreement between all the owners of the unit. This agreement can be used as a contract between individuals or be added to the agreement of any association, making the association to become a **"free association"** (FA), which then can hold the assets of, and in return to licensing to, any "normal" company, which is to be used as the "OI" (**"operating institute"**) of the many peers in the "FA".

The agreement is designed for increasing the individual power-and-flexibility of each of the "peer owners" together having more power to realize their "something" in common (- their commons). **Individual ownership is essential!** It allows tying the power of participating in association in this "commercial world" together with all the legalization and commercialization of this world; It grants the owners the power to directly evaluate their unit as a whole, by individually trading their own shares and hence keeping their power of re-evaluating their unit always instant and relevant.

This agreement is **validated by buying**, so that buyer of such ownership must first agree with the agreement and hence the agreement is stronger than any of the unit's owner/s. Per each such unit, the agreement forbids, directly or indirectly, accumulating more than one position of ownership and prevents one entity owning it all.

Being *peers for granted* when being unable to sell-it-all to some third party makes each of the peers be unable to earn from the failure of the other. It also reduces the risk's management of them as a group, when compared with the problems of to big to fall, since always they can check and balance each other, or exit, for benefiting each of them, as well as most of them remaining in their group. As such it is useful *even between competitors* at least for establishing the ground, roles and rules for their exact competition, (otherwise splitting them for controlling them is inevitable) e.g. for marketing when the peers are preferred clients of the business or on one specific room, some renters will be competitors, but when they are organized as peers against owner, they can benefit.

ComComism is a *peaceful, lawful and natural* way for *decentralization of power* in communities: It is useful for small business for getting organized against the bigger, including those "too big to fall" ones; it is a way of making business in a wise and "good manner", by e.g. benefiting preferred clients as peers; it is suitable for *stooping the infinite cycle of bailout/privatizations*, by making the government be partner with the peers being the excuse of the government to "help" the failing institutions (i.e by GovComComizing).

Type, as $d*i=c*n$;	d, as $0<d<=1$	Allowed to Sell to	Type of Community	i, as $0<i$, number of all shares	n, number of peer's shares
Scomcom	Static	Outer	Open	?	?
Icomcom	Dynamic	Inner	Closed	i=m==number of members	$0<n<=1$
Dcomcom	Dynamic	Outer/Inner	Open	i=m==number of members	$0<n<=1$

The ComComism can be used in Scomcomized units *only for open* communities, in Dcomcomized units for *first close then open* communities and in Icomcomized units *only for close* communities - after all, the comcomism is all about being content, by bringing about your ability to readjust the things you belong to, while sitting at the top of your unit with your peers and having the power coming with responsibility to satisfy yourself in your community as well as your community.

The "Credible" ones must first be Authentic in regard to their interest.

ComComized units are for you

- **if you are** activists, artists, developers, researchers, small businesses (in front of the bigger ones) and/or loyal but smart costumers or citizens (as you establish some "relationship" identifying yourself by your actions when acting more than just once in paying or voting);
- if you, as well as your peers, **want stopping** *each other from been bought for handing the whole unit* to some third party, which is normally done for betraying your unit, while modifying the initial/primary causes/interests of your unit and while removing its history and its identity; and
- if you, as anyone of the peers, **want becoming more** *powerful, free and responsible*, while benefiting the individuals as well as benefiting the collective, by
  - always preventing each of you from being unwillingly held and from accumulating more than one position per a unit and
  - at any time letting each of you (for the worse cases or for the best calculated exit) trading your position, but only with whom agree with the ComComIsm and letting all of you independently amongst yourselves to define the number of yourselves (- the peers) .

In itself, the "ComComIsm" reduces centralization, without harming the economy - in "this commercial world", with "normal" and commercial means and while helping the economy of most of the individuals. ComComism *strengthen the power of the many* on the account of the few controlling most of the resources and as such it is, or might be, threatening only these (huge) few. Centralization in economy is its top most problem, at least as long as politicians, experts or their employees, are obsessed in building their reputation for their next job in the rich/richer "house" (for more read "Winner-Take-All Politics").

- So for making *decentralization to work and for it to work exactly for you,* don't ask politicians nor experts to do your job – since their next job is in the rich/er house.
- Instead, hire them and for hiring them, although been only one and only too "small" one, first find your peers of your kind, preference and strength, then search in the Internet for "ComComIsm", look for @A@ - the personal agreement and sign it with your peers. And so after signing and as you are already ComComized with your peers, you (in small amounts/activities together) with your peers could finally hire the experts, including the lobbies, you need for serving your causes and interests, just now like company, for a longer time frame and with more solid and specified staff and plan.

Some specific examples for realizing ComComS: (More: http://tinyurl.com/qor4or)
- A ComComized pub/coffee-shop/restaurant, of which peer owners are tourists - making the peers to become offshore owners of the comcom and hence its marketers. (in Berlin, xberg).
  - **Also,** special streets, such as in old-towns could get organized against market-halls.
- A ComComized organization for protection of the interest of renters/tenants: While gathering peer owners in smaller ComComS, each per one specific region and for a specific desired balance of prices per a specific group, when these comcoms are together also peer owners in a bigger ComCom, which is able to use lobbies for the interest of the renters.
  - They could establish partnerships with real state and builders entities for reducing the renting price, also by putting mass of renters (being their peer holders) to the streets, such ComComS could have (with their lobbies) much stronger impact.
- **Also,** With all that risk of nuclear energy, why not wind-farms? Comcomized activists' group for green energy can generate **earning in their act**, while suppling the required energy and for shifting itself into the "center", such as: "we (as many different groups) can be the peer owners of windfarms and hence be earning from making the energy cleaner and risk-less".
- **Also,** banks, insurance companies and all other type of institutes of which power is only a derivative of accumulation of small power of the many, including the Govcomcom http://tinyurl.com/pnx8cx and tax release for each comcom (of which $d=1$).

Content (first incomplete edition. For more search the keyword: *comcomism*)

2. What is a ComComized unit ?

First grasp: please imagine two (concentric) rings: one (blue) inside the other (red), where the outer is cut into identical pieces - The positions in the outer ring are of "peer owners" having equal share, unlike the other owners, being the "ordinary owners", having their share in the inner ring:

- The ratio between both rings is represented by the number *d*, measuring the decentralization property of the unit, as $0<d<=1$,
    - where $d*100$ equals the percentage of the sum of all shares owned by all "peer owners" of the unit
    - and where *c* is the number of all the peers, each of which holds *n* shares and *i* is the number of all the issued shares of the unit, such that $d*i=c*n$.
- Each comcomized unit can only be one of these 3:
    - Scomcoized unit, of the type S, being open and having *S*tatic *d;*
    - Icomcomized unit, of the type I, being an *I*ndycomcomized unit and closed while having Dynamic *d;* or
    - Dcomcomized unit, of the type D, being open and having *D*ynamic *d*.
- Peer owner can only be a person or a ComComized unit of the same type as the owned unit
    - and the number of all the peer owners (the *c)* must be agreed by them independently, hence only the peers amongst themselves are to determine their number.
- Each owner shall directly, or indirectly, obtain **only one position** in the unit, where
    - the owner can sell her/his shares only to whom accepts the agreement, and the seller alone is able to determine the value, the time and the identity of the buyer in that sell unless the selling in the case of Icomcomized units is to outer entity;
    - the price in each such transaction reflects the value of the whole unit, as
        - the value of the whole unit equals *i* times the share's price in that sell.

d=0.30

What is a Scomcomized unit ? Scomcoized unit allows both type of its owners: the peer and the ordinary ones, to sell their shares to outer entities and its *d* is *unchangeable*, so that
- its *d* is defined only once, at the unit's initiation, hence its *d* is as its "DNA"; and
- its "ordinary owner" can be a person, a ComComized unit, or any other organization.
- *In this way....*
    - No representative/proxy of the peers could constantly act against their will, because at any time each of the peers can exit together with some (best achieved) return of the investment put in the unit;
    - Non of the peers could legally betray them by causing legal sell of the whole unit to a singular third party just for removing its history and/or destroying its identity;
    - The peers individually trade their position and the trading is in direct correlation to the value of the whole unit.
        - Hence each peer has a direct and instant power of re-evaluation of the whole unit – a power directly related to the peer's benefit/lost; and
    - The peers could now personally benefit by earning while gaining more of their individual power, from/by doing, realizing and/or having their common "things":
        - As now the peers directly influence, and are influenced by, the accumulated value of what they together have and do in commons related to them (-their commons).
            - which is the value of the what is resulted from their activities in common after that value is added to the value of their common resources;
        - As their responsibility for the commons is now rewarded, since it is bound with their personal benefit, which is even inheritable to their children, and is now to be set also for/by their individual and unique experiences (of trial by error, share and learn) as they are to comprehend together with the peer they preferred.

The peers' protection in Scomcomized versus the one in Icomcomized or Dcomcomized unit?
The Icomcmoized, or the Dcomcomized, unit allows outer entities entering it only by becoming its peer, unlike the Scomcomized unit allowing entrance not only to its peers, but also to its "ordinary owners" and hence allowing an entrance by skipping the independent authority of its "peer owners", which is to define their number.
- This in itself makes the Scomcomized, from all the 3 comcomized forms, to be the least protecting its peers, especially as smaller is its d. Hence making it essential to have the d in the Scomcomized units be static, so that knowing its d would tell to the outer the most about the possibilities of its balance of powers.

Why should a community become Icomcomized or Dcomcomized unit? Becoming Dcomcomized unit is for community being more open than that of the Idnycomcomized and becoming Icomcomized unit is useful for community holding and/or accumulating property, which is desired to be not transferable out of that community, when the community also desire allowing its members to trade their positions individually (e.g. for advancing groups of their representatives). Normally, that is for an autonomic or monopolistic community trying being less manipulated by its representatives. In general such community become NPO and might be
- community having a political social agenda, (http://tinyurl.com/yzujp5q)
- a community of individuals sharing their commons, typically in a large scale; http://tinyurl.com/2uwcoba ,
- a community of which the ownership over its property is desired to be free from tax,
  - e.g. (http://tinyurl.com/2wdpgqh#post-798996) when the evaluation of trading is not by money(but by vmoney or amoney), since it is done only in a state of study/game;
- a community which is to protect its properties against the outers maybe when sharing the belief that banks hold states and/or that banks and states together sit in the other side to themselves; and/or
- a state (in a constitution of its citizens http://tinyurl.com/yct8jq3),
  - as the members of the state are its citizen.

What is a Dcomcomized or Icomcomized unit? The Dcomcomized unit, unlike Icomcominzed one, allows each of its peers to trade the peer's membership with an outer entity for the price of her/his n shares, as it is defined by the peer, where the *d* in both is *changeable*, such that $d=(c*n)/i$ and $i=m$, where
- *m* is the number of all of privileged members in the unit, of which each
  - is either peer owner in the unit,
  - or one, previously being its peer owner and currently is a holder in its ordinary owner;
- each privileged member can always switch back from being non peer to being peer (and hence the unit provides a security net for its member);
- each ordinary owner must be held only by privileged members of the unit and can only be either of the same type as the owned unit, or a Scomcomized unit of which *d=1*;
- the number of issued shares is as the number of privileged members, as *i=m*;
- the value of *n* is defined only by the (authority of the) peers, where
  - *n* is bigger than *0* and the smaller or equal *1* and its default value is *1*.
- ***In this way....***
  - When the *d* of the community is yet unknown (but is not 1, nor 0), the Indycomcomized structuring is useful for self-tuning the *d*. And so, you might want to begin with an Indycomcom for self-tuning its *d* and maybe afterward becoming Dcomcom and then finally Scomcomized with a fixed *d:*
  - The Indycomcomized or the Dcomcomized unit provides to its peers **a security net** of *n* shares for the worst case, but so that, the one can swap holding from being peer, when desiring to try benefit with others some more than only those *n* shares.

- In any case, any member in the Indycomcom or Dcomcomized must **first become a peer** in it and hence the power of authority of the peers as independent unit, which is to decide their number, is stronger in the Indycomcom or Scomcom more than in the Scomcom, since the peers Independently set their n in while having full control on who could enter the unit.

What can modify the d in the Indycomcom or Dcomcom? The d can only be changed (because of $d=(c*n)/i$ or $d=(c*n)/m$) by
- the change m - reduction/growth of the number of the privileged members,
- the ratio (c/m) - privileged members' movements between being, or being not, peers and/or
- the change of n.

Why to modify the n in the Indycomcom or Dcomcom? Since $i=m$,in average each privileged member has exactly 1 share, so when $n=1$ that average is identical to the one of the peers and hence when the peers set $n<1$ they creates an advantage for the ordinary members in the unit – an advantage proportional to the decreasing of d – as smaller n as bigger advantage.
- Decreasing the value of n can be used for advancing ordinary owners by the peers. As an example, when the ordinary owners are held by proxies/representatives of some or all of the peers and are privileged members grouped together by holding an ordinary owner.

What is unit? It is an expression meant to cover any type of organization managed by/for people when working-together/managing/dealing any type of assets.

What are layers of ownership:
- *An example of layers of ownership:* if A is a 10% owner of X, owning 10% of Y, owning 10% of Z , then A is an owner of Z, although not directly, but indirectly, via X and Y,hence X and Y are another 2 layers of ownership between A and Z, such that A indirectly owns 0.1 % of Z.
- *The ownership in such layering can be horizontal or not:* It will be horizontal when all A' peers, i.e. one peer such as A, will indirectly (via her/his X', Y') own 0.1% of Z. It will be non horizontal, even when each of A , X or Y is a peer owner with exactly other 9 peer owners, when another X2 is a peer owner, as the X is in Y, but when X2 is owned by 100 peer owners, and not by 10, then each peer owners in X2 would own only 0.01% of Z, meaning only the tenth of what A owns.
- *The horizontal ownership in layering is important for* providing the peers the possibility to meet/learn/react-with each other in small groups in which they can still recognize each other and at same time being able to move as peer to other such group (e.g. when are not satisfied in the previous), but still be united and keeping the form of one big group which is necessary to implement bit enough power. Such horizontal layering provides scalability through structuring organizations in forms of comcomized units..

Stopping the endless accumulation of power being a root of evil: ComComism allows people to differ through some layers of ownership and, as an example, this can be useful for comcomizing a bank for its clients by moving their deposit to the bank they own. Also, the ComComism, per each owned unit, forbid accumulation of positions thorough all layers of ownership, and as such it can tackle the problem of representatives in massive scale, where such representatives are never personally known to (almost all) the voters, by having small groups comcomizing their units, while personally and organically being developed by equally owning their bigger ones, but still making the individuals able to move between the "small" units and keeping the unity of the bigger ones.

A one coin peer owners (coin such as Euro): This example is of only 2 layers comcoms, it suits Scomcom, Dcomcom or Icomcom and it is based on multiple and periodical payments, so that the longest payment interval of 1 coin (such as once a year) is payed by the peer owners in the (1st-layer) comcom, where all other shorter such intervals (such as monthly, weekly, daily, hourly, minutely or secondly) are payed by peers owners holding (2nd-layer) comcom being ordinary owners in the same (1st layer) comcom. Such periodical payments suit technique, such as prepay, paypal and/or bitcoins/dcoins etc. Depending on the policy/regulation established by the existing peers and in the event of new peer entrance, the new-one shall pay the payment payed by the old ones in all their previous payments, or the value of a share established in the transactions.

[----~~----]

3. Some Practical Issues:

My commitment to you: Before we continue, let me put this short commitment (and please use it at any time for to challenge me against my actions): In all issues forming the comcomism and for avoiding any conflict of interests when doing my best in providing authentic consultation,

- I shall not become an owner except of **A)** being peer owner or **B)** in the case of temporarily holding positions of ownership only for latter delivering them to peers owners.

How to ComComize?

- In very short, first commit yourself with your peers by using the following guideline (page 16,17) for making your contract with your own peers (- the peer owners) and optionally with other (ordinary) owners, each of which is (to become) an individual owner over some share over properties collectively belong to the unit (been ComComized).
- Note that directly, or indirectly, per each owner, only one position to be held in a unit is allowed - accumulation of positions in a ComComized unit is forbidden.
  - For this matter the ComComIsm LTD, as one #G *global body,* issues identity and certification and/or authorizes, as part of the 4 degrees of authorization for protecting and supporting the peer owners (the G#->#L->#P=>#U):
    - the global body (**#G**),
    - of which the (**#L**) are its authorized agents being "Localized" in different states,
    - of which the (**#P**) are the authorized agents "Providing" specific services/product
    - to their (**#U**), being the people or bodies "Using" such services/products.
- Note that the for the Scomcomized unit the ratio (the d) of the potion held by the peers is unchangeable after been set, so you should take the necessary deep consideration as for this ratio before setting it or after it is set before taking your position in such unit.
  - Ask yourself this: "Do I want to accumulate power?" - if so I am an ordinary owner, otherwise a peer owner, and then "what is the d and with whom do I want to partner"?

The 3 levels for comcomizing a unit: (also see figure-1)

- The Personal Agreement ("PA") between individuals (the 7 th chapter),
- The Free Association ("FA"), turning a "normal" association into a comcomized one
- The Operating-Institute ("OI"), of an "FA" designed for holding "normal" companies.

The Free Association (FA) is the most essay way for expanding or large groups to create a comcomized unit (in the form of Scomcom, Icomcom or Dcomcom), were the agreement establishing comcomized unit is embedded in the agreement of the association, such that

- the association would let its members to trade their membership, by having each of its members agreeing to the "personal agreement" and
- the membership of each member is tradable, where the total value of the association (its "T") equals the sum of the value of membership of all its members.

Note that the membership of peer owners has equal value unlike the one of ordinary ones.

The Operating Institute (OI) of the "FA" is any ("normal") company, if instead of the company owning some or all of its assets, it is the "FA" which owns the assets and which grant a license for the use to the company in some conditions, such as of specific use and assignments in the company and for specific period of time etc.

Figure-1: the 3 levels for comcomizing a unit:

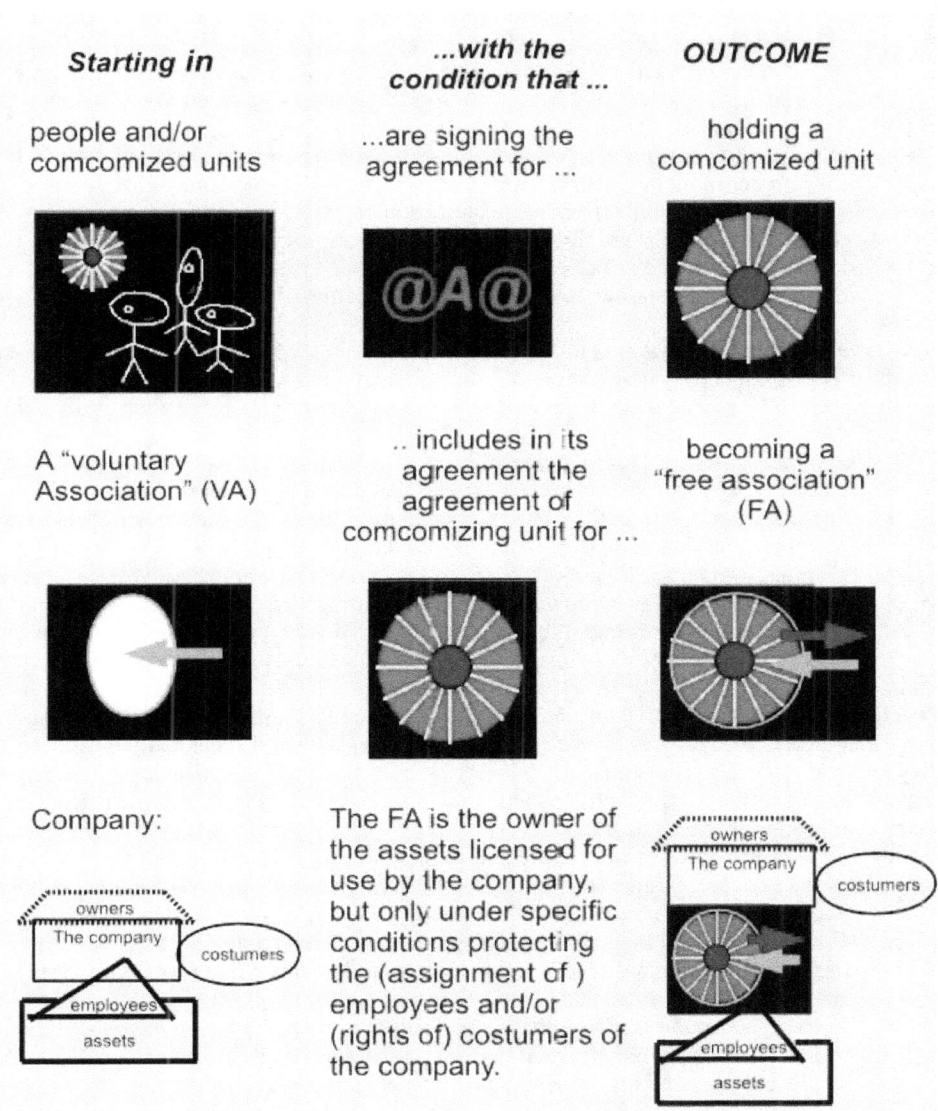

The Comcomism ltd, here as an example or a use-case, functioning as one #G:
- Only the "ComComIsm activists" in group of 20 to 100 can together create a Scomcom of which d=1 and which is entitled to invest in the ComComIsm LTD. For becoming a "comcomism activist" one should be doing something for comcomism: e.g. book buyer.
- The ComComIsm LTD also authorize and/or provide on-line services for ComComized units, as well as workshops in 4 levels for issues related to ComComIm for:
    - **A)** Gathering on the ground in groups, each having its own special interest/goal/origin etc, so that we would become diverse, even though being united in some aspects being related to ComComism; and
    - B) Learning and exchanging experiences and practices in such specific group of some specific or general issues related to getting being organized in a ComComized units.
- The comcomism ltd has its total value be constant (say 4m or more), as the price per one member of Scomcom is constant and cheap (with possibilities for high dividend), where the number of members times price per member= price per comcomized-unit, until the conditions for well diversity and localization per each state are accomplished, such that when the conditions are fulfilled then the comcomism ltd is to be comcomized.
- In the last page of this book you can find how we, the "ComComIsm activists", are going to even earn while growing in multiple organizations.

How to arrange peer's payments to be periodically and in small amounts? So that the entry of new peer is conditioned by first completing the payment required to be equal to the one done by the existing peers. The payment can be in equivalent to money such as in activities or in "real" money.

What kind of peers - some example please?
- Authentic activists, artists, developers, researchers and/or contributes;
- Organization based on distribution of content in the public such as in open-source, cc etc.
- Members and donors in organizations based on donation;
- The many when are loyal but clever renters/byers/borrowers/employees/citizens in front of the few ones, such as landowners/sellers/creditors/employers/political-communities
    - and as those few ones are in front those alike which are simply now the bigger ones;
- Small business straggling against other nearby such business and/or the bigger ones;

Practical issues in General: The comcomism can serve members in a list (like mailing list owned by its members), to be organized in a more authentic, scalable and organically developed form, as they are peer owners having equal share over (the body having) the means by which they are organized, so that their organization is able to realize an effective longterm plans (for, say, the 5 years to follow) for their interest only.
- *Such means* can be from simple mailing list, to properties located in the real world, until assets such as of banks (manging finance institutes) and such as of states (manging licensing and resources such as minerals).
- *Such plans* can include all the necessary means of production for achieving the goals of the peers, such as stores, services and servers with domains name (even with ISP and starlights etc) and local addresses and means for transportation.
- Such *organization* is more likely to be focused more on bettering its *authenticity*, which can be good for *marketing* itself, its services and/or products - Example:
    - A comcomized unit of which peer owners are power producers (such peers as *artists, activists (e.g against nuclear energy), journalist, developers, researchers, inventors* etc), which is a partner with investors and/or existing strategic commercial company in another comcomized unit of which peers are *preferred consumers.* (see figure-5)
    - Costumers organized as peer owners of the organization caring for their interest -
        - they can be renters or buyers seeking for bettering their conditions.

- *This holds even* when yet any *set of values couldn't* be sufficient for becoming a base for gathering upon it a long lasting, big and strong enough group, but still and instead, when a *set of rules could* be sufficient.
  - The comcomizing rules are doing just that:
  - What for? realizing social objectives serving many small groups which otherwise are contradicting or hostile each other, for establishing cooperation between them, since for any one thing (e.g. a room) upon which two or more (e.g. renters) are to compete, still there are a lot of things to do for improving their conditions for getting what they are compete upon. The renters in front of the landlords, need good law consulting, better pricing, lobbing, market researching and influence on the market, by buying and selling some special cases, for *benefiting* themselves: the *participants in competition.*
  - For example (and take the berlin-tempelhof as a an example for the followings), for social matter being handled badly and which is already used commercially:
    - Comcomizing the project is significant for establishing one big group, big enough to be well united and active for long terms (say next 5 yeas), where in realty and instead there are only many small groups, each can be organized for benefiting its members and some together can be peer owners in another bigger comcom for realizing some aspect, plans and/or simply getting the required information. This can work even when each of the groups has its own special (and contradicting) interest and plan in that area. More ever, since so many members are directly involve in it, also a political power is bind to it and such groups could be devolved together with some social sides/aspects as the equality is protect in any comcomized unit. Comcomizing the group even as some individuals are living it and some new are entering it, could make group working for very long terms, maybe even with an office serving some such groups together and maybe as those groups are comcomized too.
- *A grate impact – political, social and commercial one*, can be achieved, when large number of peer owners are orchestrated and active (e.g. on demonstration), for their individual interest matching the interest of their comcomized group. *Think of one big bank of which clients are its peer owners and see the political social impact of it.*

[----~-----]

4. Some Principal Issues:

What Comcomizing units is good for? Get organized while realizing equality in commercial world
- between peers joining together for achieving their common "goals" and "dreams" providing a bridge to their goals from this world as it is set by the current rules.
- It is useful for building up a new *commercial* power of peers *being* owners and free, yet building up a massive, organic, authentic and more sustainable power of the many.

What ComComism brings to the peers for having their representatives satisfying them better *(when compared with another systems for equal voting rights)?* Their independence right to trade their rights (at least for providing an automatic minorities' protections) -
- A right to be independent from any policy made in the unit, by breaking up from the unit, where the voting right itself together with all other rights of the peer are trade-able,
  - such that the value of the rights of the peer is able to be bargain for the best positive return for the investment made/put by the individual peer to/in the unit and
    - such that the value of the rights directly reflects the value of the unit a whole.

The blood and the skin in organizations of the people: Equality between peers can, and should, be realized by both type of bottom-top organizations:
- the self-organized/democratic organizations regulating how to position things in that body and hence functioning as their body's blood and
- the ComComized units regulating how to go out of and into that body and hence functioning as their body's skin.

The power of the legs *(generated by the independence right of the peers to trade their rights)* specifically ***against bad and corrupted representation:*** (see interview http://tinyurl.com/2wkzujx)
- ***First - the problem is of being ignored:*** Many times we find that our power in voting, or our voice, is ignored - hence we are ignored! This is normally done -
  - by restricting complex policies, such as
    - when, where, by whom and in what form shall we be heard;
  - amid pumping and orchestrating, around our voices, a strong mixture of Spams and spins attracting most of the attention in the air(e.g. wars near election time);
  - and while other issues are always pushed up as we are kept uncaring, helpless and/or confused (disoriented), while still, our representative claim to act in our name,
    - while keeping their power, such that our voice shall be constantly (mis)interpret.
- **The solution - keeping the option of leaving being relevant and regulated in a respectful manner**: Such that in a comcomized organization, each of the peers in any moment has not only our power in voting (by voice), but also the power of leaving the organization (by legs). This (regulated) new (leg) power allows:
  - each peer to effect the value of the organization as a whole and
  - each peer to exit with a positive value of the return for the investment put in the unit.
- **Hence, by providing each peer with additional power of ownership,** the model makes stronger the power of each of the peers being equal and of all of them as a group in front of their representatives. Such peer's individual power of ownership is, in essence, the power to sell the share, at any time and price and to any buyer who agrees with the model.
- This new "legs power" in itself **forces the collective and its representatives to better satisfy the individuals having the powe**r.
  - so that each owner, not only has the power of (equal or non-equal) "voice" in occasionally voting (which is always constrained by the policy enforced in the unit), but also the power of the "legs" to leave the unit at any time and with a positive return of the investment put in the unit.

An illustration for the power of the legs: Please imagine that a "new Hitler" is now, by "democratic means", start ruling Germany and that Germany is a comcomized unit.
- Now, suppose we, you and me, were actually voting for her/him and suppose we did not, or could not, understand and that we simply believed that s/he is the one best fitting for fighting for our cause, the cause of the "working (German) class" (didn't he claim so?) and then, after some time, we could better understand that s/he is actually doing "things" we could never support
  - (e.g. burning the parliament's house and accusing for that a "polish" one).
- Well, any farther moment from the moment we understood, we are signed on the actions s/he did in our name, so that every thing s/he did in our name is in our (your and mine) personal responsibility! Why?
  - Because each of us always could leave with a return for our investment in that unit.
- Such is the kind of responsibility and power any owner in any comcomized unit has the kind of ownership being a matter of choice, to be able at any moment to leave with a return to the investment put in the unit.

What the model comes to solve? The issue of over accumulation of (an inheritable) power!

- Only as peers we could care the best for our common interest, but in any big enough democratic collective we often cannot trust any of our representatives and harder is the struggle for keeping our representatives more trustful, as larger is the scale or bigger is the power of "our" collective - Why?
  - ○ Because our voting power is always limited (to what, when, how and about what to vote). Sometimes the representatives do the opposite of what we want as they are escaping liability. Often we cannot leave, and if we can leave we could do it only "naked", taking with us nothing of our investment in term of work/time/money etc.
- The origin of the problem is that in any democratic collective when the peers constitute their collective, they are additionally requested, for becoming equal in the power adding up the collective, *to giveaway their individual power (of ownership)*, by which each of them can liberate her/his self from the mistakes done by the collective.
  - ○ An illustration of this problem: As we try neutralizing the possibilities of takeover the commons (so that "normally", our "common things" are to be found, supply and/or be democratically used in the non-commercial side of our living),
    - and so we find that the non-commercial aspects are only temporarily respected until some "fruits" from that "common pool" are privatized and/or commercialized, (e.g. bailout until sell/privatizes) but now only for the benefit of some few delivering (e.g. by banks) the commons to the many, in the name and on the account of the rest.

What protection ComComIsm provides? The protection is of neutralizing attempts of taking it over (- by making itself, for the others, a bad-pill to take and, within itself, by the use of the independence right of its peers generating its peers' power of the legs against bad representation):

- This is significant for the authenticity of people and/or organizations, which are to work together in long term, while putting much efforts for realizing their "common things"as they produce, serve and/or hold some valuable properties;
- This is significant in this capitalistic environment having its ways to buy people/organizations, if/when are standing in the capitalist 's way to "grow its bodies",
  - ○ as the grow only by following only these these 3 steps:
    - first *takeover* some elements, of which each is a small body or business,
    - then *pack* these elements such that you could
    - finally *hand it over* as a new product for higher price to the richer;
- This protection confines the power of investor, donors or cooperations, while turning them visible ones when cooperating with them only in a fixed balance of powers – the balance between the peers getting the investment and the investors/donors,
  - ○ it is a protection specifically against donors or cooperations, who would start essay for afterward isolating the receivers and then, while putting new conditions for receiving the next donation, undercover and in the shadow, influencing and controlling those (activists) realizing their cause, while learning their how-to and impact, for latter being first at creating a new market in alignment with their learning about the cause and even against the receiving organization.
- This is significant in ComComs' stock marketing against the terrible instability appearing in the ordinary stock marketing, when is made by few producing massive putt/call options able to cause lost of tenth of the value of the whole market in less than five minutes,
  - ○ since when the bodies are comcomized and the trading is in comcoms' stock marketing, many individuals should have been required for preforming an equivalent massive act.

The Peaceful and Balanced approach this model takes: This model *confines* a balance of powers between the peer owners versus the (non-peers aka) ornery owners and hence, even though being self-protected from being taken over, still it lets the non-peer a confined position together with the peers. This confined balance, while being fixed in the Scomcomized units, or dynamic one in the D/Icomcomized unites, provides a peaceful way for the rich/risky (as non-peers) and for the poor/cautious (being the peers) to approach each other in the same frame, sitting at its (own) top and integrating both types of personal ownership.

- The Scomcomized unit allows ordinary owners (such as investors, donors and governmental, ngo, association, non-compressional or compressional entities etc) together with the peers to establish a partnership in ownership, but only with a restrictive balance of powers *defined only once* in its initiation when setting the decentralization property *(the d)* of the owned unit.
  - As such the balance of power between the peers and the ordinary owners of the unit is a long time transparent balance allowing new participant to the unit to make their (better) choice.
  - In other words, the unit is balanced and the measure of itself being balanced (*the d*) is fixed and transparent.

The model's principles: The model can easily be established between the owners of the unit by signing on a 17 points contract, where the contract forbids to deliver any share of the unit to whom disagree with this contract. Compared with other models - this model is more balanced and diverse in the positions able to possess it and/or cooperate in/with it -

- The contract establishing it *lasts even beyond the time held by its current owners;*
- It regulates the *free swapping of ownership*, such that each owner, as in shareholding, can
  - **A)** effect the value of the whole unit reflected by the price of the share in the transaction made by the one and
  - **B)** exit the unit together with a positive value made in such transaction - the return value for the investment put into the unit (in terms of time, money and otherwise);
- It allows the peers holding it to be *organically developed as a group,*
  - due to their *independent authority* to set their number;
- It establishes *the boundaries of the autonomy of the peers*, due to its decentralization property (- the *d*, as *100 times d* equals the percentage held together by all the peers), thereby allowing both type of owners coexisting in a peaceful, regulated and transparent manner, whatsoever is the amount put into the unit by investors, donors or lenders, which are normally the non-peers owners,
  - either in the case of D/Icomcom, where the *d is dynamic*, as any power in it must first past the power of the peers and last fall to it and as the trading of its shares is internal and only optionally external,
  - or in the case of Scomcom, as it first integrates and then restricts a clear and *fixed balance of powers* between the peers and another non-peer (aka o-owners) holding it – no matter what is the peers' number or the value of the unit as a whole;
- It disable accumulation of shares in the unit so that
  - **A)** *directly, or indirectly,* each of its owner has **only one position** in it,
  - **B)** there is *no one position which could ever take the whole of it,* and
  - **C)** each peer's position can only be held by either comcomized unit or a person,
- **and hence** it is made undesirable for those who hold things only for exclusivity or bodies which are used to grow in these 3 steps:
  - 1st: taking over some elements, while removing the history of each,
  - 2nd: packing these elements for to hand over the pack as a new product for higher price to the richer
  - and 3rd: handing it over.

Conclusion: This model is far more beneficial for those who can organized as peers, especially for peers in self organizations, as it regulates the property of their organization as their individual ownership over that property.

- It works better for peers sharing common interest/goals/causes and/or who find themselves in front of common threats.
- It allows the peers to work with non peer at its the top most level.
- It scale up from 2 peers and above and
- as a type of organizations it opens new ways for cooperation, even between competitors, who still have to establish the game and themselves as player in it for their own common interest in their competition.

[----~~~----]

5. Some examples of use:

The comcomism in daily ordinary living: Normally, as one is simply carrying through her/his choices and actions, the one establishes some "relationship" identifying the one as part of a group. Such group can become a free association (FA) for simply bettering the conditions of its peers owners, where such choices/actions can be buying/supporting "something", or opposing it, or when getting organize to realize, to sell or to vote for/against it, or when trying guarding some properties. Examples for such choices/actions in such "relationships" can be found

- In "simple" reading specific newspaper, buying in specific shop/market-wall or choosing the main media to trust when listening to via internet/tv channels, social-networking, news, search engine etc. E.g
  - **Comcomized media of press and/or news agencies**, of which each serves and answers the many queries of its peer owners by its (unified) subjects roles. The media sells true rather than sexy stories, each story is only initiating, querying or answering in only one of the three criteria: reports (in realty), opinions (of the authors) or issues (not report nor opinion). The clients of the media are its readers and its peer owners. The media maintains coherent archive, which is open to its peers. The peers are able to submit and edit reports or opinions, as well as to reflect to issues and to open new issues. The subjects roles, such as editors are able in addition to the role of the peers also to close or categorize issues for reflecting the unique simplified tune of the specific media for guiding the readers with their interpretation observation and opinion;

Turning the power of consumption to the power of ownership. In the power (of choice in consumption) of customers and citizens treated as customers can be used by them when are organized as comcomized group for realizing long plans and long standing activities - making them as peer to be loyal but smarter costumers or citizens. E.g:

  - **Citizens of the city opposing nuclear energy** becoming peer owners owning their wind-farms or any other massive green power factories, such as those electricity produced from solar, geothermal, biogas, biomass, and low-impact small hydroelectric sources.
  - **ComCom Social:** http://tinyurl.com/274ponz social networking of which members are its peer owners.
  - **comcomized mailing list:** http://tinyurl.com/yzu72yy mailing list of which members are its peer owners.
  - **Comcomizing bank:** people can comcomize a bank for their selves by moving their deposit to it and still be differ through some layers of ownership (see "A one coin peer owners").

ComComized Donation: http://tinyurl.com/y6v2usd activists as peer and as the ordinary are group being Scomcomed on d=1 and of which peer are donors paying the same amount. By the way, spiritual effort cannot any more be separated from other side of leaving – those involve material ownership in this commercial world.

Self organization of small business: e.g. helping businesses in one street to be more attractive than those in another street (other small businesses) or more attractive than marketwall *other big business) http://tinyurl.com/36sztvy .

ComCom communities: http://tinyurl.com/2uwcoba , many small groups can be ComComS, each is a peer owner in one bigger ComCom acting as their proxy/representative for bigger and more general issues, especially in the lack of one set of values gathering all the people for long period commitments . (e.g. on Tempelhof see more in the end of the book).

Comcomized Grassroots movements: Becoming peer owners over the property of organization of grassroots movement can change for better their destiny such that none of the movmement's members could hand it over and some times such that the members could gain personal benefit from boosting the movement, which can attract new members (e.g. nuclear power activists could build wind farms owned by cities peer owners).
Grassroots "movements" should always carry on and have more than only one successful step of successfully achieving any specific agenda, after which the "movement" is "normally" falling apart. Here is an example for what comcomizing could do by simply having the malling list being owned by the members in the list:
- *http://tinyurl.com/yzujp5q* - the mailing lists of 13 million members on barackobama.com (now ofa - "organizing for america") is a showcase for a failure in organizing a grassroots movement, although succeeding in realizing one step in such movement. A showcase for activists of any kind! Specially for the antiwar ones! The obama mailing list is now dead!
  - If that mailing list was comcomized, such that its members are also its peer owners, then he, very near after being elected, could never kill it by transferring its ownership to the principal body governing the democratic party. And yes sure he now need some of the 13m member of it and yes sure many of them are against many things he does, and could, if the movement was comcomized, also be split and create a contra movement to the obamas, but still as both are grassroots ones.

Govcomcoming for breaking the cycle of bailout/privatization: GovComCom is a ComCom of which ordinary owners are governments and/or their agencies and of which peer owners are the needy becoming the excuse or reason for the government/s to sell (privatize) to , and/or to buy/ credit/ guarantee/ bailout, some bodies acting as monopolies or big cooperation.
- Normally governments use excuses for benefiting those bodies and the excuses can be translated to list of of people (of that interest), to which the government is to try to help by such act. These people should become peer owners, for breaking the cycle of sell to and then buy from those monopolies. More *http://tinyurl.com/pnx8cx* .

The Stability of peer owners' market: The power of the many, of which each has a full control over her/his interests, not only protect the one or the many as a group, but also stabilize their actions in their individual concern over their interests. This is way the stronger is the middle class in a society the more stable is that society and when it comes to comcomized units this emerges as the higher is the c and d in each comcomized unit, the more stable tend to be the value of such alternative units. And similarly, the market based on more such comcomized units tend to be less depended on few individuals being in the fire to get some earning (and fast).

This is because of the higher dependency on more players evaluating for their own benefit the values of such units, while having a wider/deeper check and balance in their evaluation, since they are in the same position as their peers (which would "normally" be those who would pull the others to follow just for latter to trick the followers). In short - the market based on comcomized units is in average more stable.

- Such comcomized units could be companies such as banks.
- This can contribute to bigger stabilization of the market and for the authenticity of the values in trading in it.
- This could also reduce running capital out of states or war of currencies.
- This is more required, as higher is the friction based on constant wrong evaluations (aka correction of the market), as the trust in banks is in decline as their success is on the account of the others and with increasing instability in political/economical warfares.

ComComized states: Constitution of its citizens constitutes one or more sub-constitutions, of which each is the formal law's foundation of one political unit such as state acting as a ComCom, where the ownership over all the resources of each such state is distributed equally between all its citizens been its peer owners and is an exchangeable privilege for another such privilege in another such state as the value of such privilege define the value of such state. This, i believe, is the final way to defend against the few taking hold on state and their resources by means of corruption, lobbies and educational, market and media control. http://tinyurl.com/qor4or#Constitution-of-its-citizens .

Who has who the banks the states or vise-versus ?
- Take Ireland and Iceland for instant, take the lost of 10% of the market in just 5 minutes which could never be done if the companies of that stock market were comcomized with significant c and d, simply because of the massive secret coordination of put/call options of so many peer owners involved in such action.
- Take the fed argumentation for lending $9 trillions to few huge banks in the 2008 crisis: "It prevented falling of the economy - such as in those times prior to world wars...The fed even latter on earn from that." http://tinyur..com/38pzbjj#post-944153
  - How can it be that all the citizens of the USA, which are the real payers for the bailout and are surely to suffer inflation, are not the peer owners of those banks receiving those $9t? (here is the proposition: http://tinyurl.com/36e4k2m)
  - As peer owners they might even choose not to sell, but at any rate those huge banks will never again could be owned only by those few who posses them only for latter coming to suck the government again.
    - And this is essential for *breaking the cycle of bailout/privatization.* (e.g. helping to stop bailout just for latter privatization in ipo such as gm.).

How to ComComize a bank? Take some people (say 5000), each deposits more than minimum amount (say $1000) having all agreed with the comcomizing agreement for establishing a bank of which clients are also its peer owners using their deposits for claiming their peer ownership - here is an example for such structuring:
- The bank is a Scomcomized unit of which d is very small and of which peer owner's value is very cheap (say $1),
  - where first day clients of the bank can become such peer
  - and where such peer can switch position to be peer owner in another Scomcomized unit of which $d=1$ and of which peer's deposit is similar in its volume (is in the same category) and which holds ornery owner position in the bank aside with other such Scomcomized unit and with other owners of the bank such as its original founders.
- This way the bank can be attractive to new customers , saying something like, *first before trusting us please be owner with us only only then put your trust and money in us* etc.

- The categories are made so that Scomcom of many peers of small input could balance Scomcom of few peers of big input, meaning in the bank those how put 1k could get privileges proportional to the number of them not only to their input.

For Whom Is The Knowledge Making Profit, *or why big cooperation put so much money in open-source projects? - (* http://tinyurl.com/yzvkm6x *e.g. 87% of linux's code is written by cooperation and not by individuals)*
- This question is for power producers! I mean for those who could/should produce the changes any society must constantly make for keeping its health - such are a ***activists, artists, developers and/or researchers***. Although the following is formulated specifically for developers (-*the geeks*), you can find the same appearance of loosing the aspects of rights over properties of the individual for latter on taking these rights be held by the big cooperation even against the set of beliefs or interest of the individuals.
  - The open-source (OSI,OSD) is one of the Spin-off of GeekNet Inc (NASDAQ:GKNT), The Open Source (OSD) added, to the simple obligation to let access to the source code of the product being distributed, additional 10 measures, all of which must comply with their definition for "the distribution terms of open-source software". The 6th, of those the 10 measures is
    - "No Discrimination Against Fields of Endeavor".
  - This measure allows Microsoft, as any other business, or weapon producers to benefit from the code you would distribute as an "open source", such that they, could benefit from it, even against your will, by learning and testing the products of your code, just for later on closing it and "improving" it to satisfy their own unknown will.
  - As for weapon producers, I learned that the killer is not the last to be responsible for the death and that the responsibility goes also to his/her officers, up to the most higher ones and to all the weapon dealers and producers making that killing possible.
    - Sorry California and sorry GeekNet inc, but you could not benefit me that much to lose my values or dignity as a thinker or a scientist -
  - For me there is no much of science or thinking in massive theft, only great impact and great control by fews. For me there is no any justification for the existence of those *businesses benefiting* from *war making, torturing or war games – war, it isn't sexy!*

The comcomized geek vs the geeknet inc hand of the open source: When d<1 the ordinary owners are strategic partner, investors, users ,tester of product made in platform. If you, power producer, are tired of acting against the interest or set of beliefs of yourself try Scomcomized geek - You can first commit yourself with your peers in a comcomized units and only then go to produce.

	d	mission	holdings	board of
GeekNet,Inc. (NSDAK:GKNTD)	0	open licensing such as of open source used in developers' platforms	Holds 5 developers' platforms; 127 employees; $13.8M market cap ;	9 directories-each has key position in another big institute;
SComCo mized Geek	?0 < d<=1?	peer ownership over developers' platforms	Held by its peer owners being Scomcomized on d=1 networks, of which p-owners-members;	?

Btw, what is your opinion on the Dna researchers (after knowing about Monsanto)? Would you feel safe to develop something in this field? What about the nano or clean tech? Isn't it satisfying only the few on the account of the many? Are you really sure that what you developed would be used only for the "good", and if not and after knowing the power of the technology. what is your responsibly for its destruction?   [----~18~----]

6. *Me and the model* (personal voice): - In our capitalistic era, it is so common and well known that any person or thing has a price, at least at a certain time - if and when some (very) influential (and hostile or friendly) player would show an interest. As a result, no one can really trust the other for never selling the whole unit in which both are (fruitfully) acting. The fact that the comcomismm eliminates such legal sell-all-option makes an argument either against it or for it and as such making it a litmus test, testing the authenticity of partners. This is the main argument for using comcomism and this is where the story of my life led me to.

Me? A poet! I am a poet, experiencing and interesting in issues such as: the relationships between objects and subjects, the dynamic distinction between existences and non-existences, the referable and non-referable types of negations, the inclusion and been included as forms of being with (which are distinguished by priorities in accessing/conditioning-existence-of one by the other) and ways beyond hierarchies to organize things - hierarchies in which i find the human being thinking and living.

In my life, for proving my arguments and for finding and sharing alternative ways to think, i invented a system providing much more efficient structuring than those of hierarchies - the pile system, breaking while building hierarchies, by recursively having the object relating two objects to be also be able to be related by any other such system's object.

I programed this system alone, for proving that when it gets to its mature state it could serve many purposes even those of our very big brothers. Since my personal purpose in inventing it, was "sharing with others alternative ways of thinking", any option of closing it in exclusive licensing could never severe my purpose and the same goes for letting it be used by any of our big brothers.

Eventually this invention was opened sourced when i was mistreated for greed, (and now you already know the geeknet inc hand of the open source face), but only after it was evaluated in a very high price for being licensed in exclusive manner (I talk about non formal evaluation of "people" from microsoft, hp and others). And yes I was in some "labs" in the "valley" and Canada and yes mysteriously there they are all full of fear of something they are coining as "being contaminated". Question: Would you mistreat your peer for a very high price and would you mistrust me or your peer for doing the same?

Today as the founder of the concept I am holding (hopefully with you) the company comcomism LTD in London.

My position as a founder of comcomism is as a consultant and not of foundation of a uniform and/or central organization, while pushing for a diverse and growing from multiple centers. That is why I do not ask for your trust or you to follow me, but instead that you would trust yourself in your organization and/or in the organization you are founding and yes it is clear to me that such organizations could be contradicting each other or even hostile one to the other.

Realizing comcomism might take more than your/mine lifetime. but in this long way at any step we can already be protected from been taken over, by being purified from pretending contributers.

Here are some links about me (http://tinyurl.com/yc58fr7) and my personal story:
- http://tinyurl.com/y8kenyv An Open Letter To Ralf Westphal
- http://tinyurl.com/2uc9cyr My first blog for starting breaking the "pile systems" inc
- http://tinyurl.com/2vdny4j An Open Public Letter to the "Pile Systems" on omadeon
- http://tinyurl.com/2czublv Pile Technology on isiwth info
- http://tinyurl.com/4933m8v#piletech The "piletech" on "organizing things"

7. The Personal Agreement for any "ComComized" Ownership: http://tinyurl.com/yhx2ryz :
This is a guideline for any personal agreement of ownership between all the owners of a unit being "comcomized", where the unit (aka a Common Company, ComCom or a comcomized unit) can only be one of the following three: Scomcomized, Icomcomized or Dcomcomize unit and each owner can only be:

- either a p-owner (Peer Owner) or a o-owner (Ordinary Owner), [1]
  - where each p-owner can only be either a person or a ComCom [2]
  - and each o-owner can only be either a person or an organization, [3]
- but only as, directly or indirectly - through any other entity, the owner obtain only one position of ownership in the unit [4] and the owner can at any time trade[5] her/his share in exchange for a valuable thing, but only as the exchange is made with whom already agreed with this agreement and is not made between an outer entity and owner in IcomCom or an outer entity and o-owner in DcomCom,
  - where the value of the thing being traded (aka the value a share) is a proportional value reflecting the value of the ComCom as a whole, such that d/c (d divided by c) is the exact share owned by each p-owner, [6]
  - where c (being the count of all p-owners, as c is bigger than one) is the exact number of all p-owners in such ComCom,[7]
  - where d (being the decentralization property of the organization and as zero is smaller than d and d is smaller than or equal to one) is unchangeable in all the lifetime of the Scomcom, unlike in DcomCom or Icomcom[8]
    - where $d * 100$ (d multiplied by 100) is the percentage of the sum of the shares held by all p-owners together, [9]
    - where $(1-d)*100$ $((1-d)$ multiplied by 100) is the percentage of the sum of the shares held by all o-owners together, [10]
      - and as $t=(v*c)/d$, (as t equals the product of v multiplied by c after the product is divided by d) [11], where
        - t is the Total reflected value of the ComCom as a whole,
        - v is the Value being trade-able for becoming a p-owner,
        - c is the Count number of exiting p-owners,
      - and hence n is the number of shares held by each p-owner, where the number of all issued shares is i, as $n=(i*d)/c$,
  - and where Dcomcomized unit, unlike Icomcominzed one, allows each of its peers to trade the peer's membership with an outer entity for the price of her/his n shares, as the price and who is the buyer is defined by the peer, where in each of both - the Dcomcomized or Icomcominzed unit, the d is *changeable*, such that $d=(c*n)/i$ and $i=m$, where
    - m is the number of all of privileged members in the unit, of which each
      - is either peer owner in the unit,
      - or one, previously being its peer owner, and currently is a holder in its ordinary owner;
    - each privileged member can always switch back from being non peer to being peer (and hence the unit provides a security net for its member);
    - each ordinary owner must be held only by privileged members of the unit and can only be either of the same type as the owned unit, or a Scomcomized unit of which $d=1$;
    - the number of issued shares is as the number of privileged members, as $i=m$;
    - the value of n is defined only by the *authority of the peers*, where
      - n is bigger than 0 and the smaller or equal 1 and its default value is 1.

- Only the *the authority of the peers* (as one group) may independently determine the number of the peers (the *c*) in a comcomized unit, [12]
  - as the type (majority of, all of or other the part of the p-owners) of the decision which must be taken for the *authority of the peers* to take into effect must be unchangeable in the lifetime of the comcom and be known to all owners; [13]
- All decisions upon any property owned by the ComCom must be either be authorized by the decisions made in a specific procedure known to all owners or be decided in it, where the procedure includes the followings: [14]
  - **Type of presence:** answering should those who vote meet online, in person, via representative, or otherwise, if otherwise then what? [15]
  - **Length of Issuing:** answering what is the length of time between rising an issue for voting (for gathering opinion of the owners upon the issue and spreading the information related to that issue) and defining the last voting time for decision (for making it valid in the name of the ComCom), so that the owners can vote upon the issue in all the time defined by the Length of Issuing, [16]
  - **Procedure of voting:** answering what is the procedure of making decision: who must be present at it and as it is starting in what, ending in what and what are the steps in between its start and its end, which must be included and what are those which should never be included, such that in its end: the issue would become either valid or invalid to represent or to be act in the name of the ComCom. [17]

Footnotes:

1. Unlike the o-owners all the p-owners have and can only have equal share.
2. This p-owner's limitation, which do not allow non comcom organizations to take a p-owner position, constitutes asymmetric conditions for protecting the peers (many) versus the non-peers (few), since ComCom in itself is an organization and in correlation to what/who can be o-owner.
4. This is for providing protection against manipulations made when playing from far by unknown identifies which mostly done as an hostile act against the distinctions made above.
5. The ability to trade the share constitutes the freedom of the individuals from any law made by the collective. Therefore, This freedom is the up most privilege granted to the individuals in the collective. It is here assumed that when having such freedom, better is the evaluation evaluating the collective, when, in the act of transactions, the evaluation is done by the individuals in the collective and versus the others out of the collective. This is why we also believe that comcomism is the most peaceful way to go.
6. $0 < v/t = d/c < 1$, where $t > 0$, $c > 1$ and $0 < d <= 1$.
12. Since always such entry of new p-owner is on the account of the old ones and hence the o-owner having the same number of shares as any p-owner will earn more than the p-owner, any such event must be approved by the p-owners and independently from the o-owners. This must be in the power of the group of the p-owners and hence its authority must be established and hereby is constituted for having *a new type of check and balance* between the peer and non-peer (ordinary) owners. With this new authority the p-owner compared with a o-owner, when both have the same number of shares are better balanced. All this must be done because: It is the peers (many) which somewhat must agree with the development of the collective, especially as such development cost their price and even if the development is for the good of the collective.
13. The measure for establishing such authority to act in the name of the group must be transparent, thereby known and be unchangeable.
14. The owners, the o-owners together with the p-owners and each relative to the proportion of the share the one holds, are the top decider ones over any property held by the organization and hereby the way to practice making such decisions is established.
17. The length from rising any issue time and until the last voting time.

No footnote : 3. 7. 8. _9._10. 11._15. and 16.

8. The 4 quick arguments (to be given for summarizing this book): Because, only as peer owners we/you could really make the changes we/you dream and demand! Make your commitment with your peers of which amount is to be defined by them, do it for your own common and personal benefits and interests, do it for strengthening the peers sharing similar weaknesses and do it while bringing additional commercial power back to the people being the peers of your kind:

- *A) One Alone Can Never Hold It* – *You-Cannot-Buy-Us-By-Buying-One-Or-Few-Of-Us:*
- *since* one owner alone could never legally possess it the unit becomes a bad-pill-to-take for the "big ones", who normally seek to *pay any required price* (to buy a person or unit) for gaining the ability to delete or harness the history and identity of the unit, by first having together with their allied a single ownership over the unit and then putting it under their wings (for their expanding). And hence
    - It is a good management of risk to be reallied always on many and never only on one and this in itself protects the peers from any false participation (to a cause) which is done only in order to (been bought for to) betray its cause.
- *B) Each Can Sell The Share As The One Wants* – *Yes-You-May-Have-Me-In-But-Only-When-I-Have-My-Way-Out!:*
- *since* each of the peers owning it can, by selling the share (of the investment put in it), exit from it together with a return value, and doing so exactly when the one desires.
    - Hence constantly and by the forces of the free market (but with the exception of the inability of each peer to accumulate shares of the same unit), such exits automatically redefine the value of its whole (as it is reflected by each such transaction of selling the share of each such peer).
    - So, its representatives must constantly (and well) satisfy the peers (been represented) and beyond any policy they might simply force with or without some excuses!
        - the problem of system of representative is when it is too big, since for having good choice those who decide who would be the representative and how should they represent must first at least know the optional selected ones, and as the bigger is the system the possibility to know the optional representatives become non-relevant, and so then the system is depended on its media for mere informing the so who control the media controls the system and mostly that is for the benefit of the few not the many been represented (e.g. italay) and system the selected Since the bigger are the systems based on representatives are proven to fail on issue of caring for the interest of the represented
- *C) It Lasts Longer Than Each Participant* – *It-Takes-Stronger-Than-Each-Participant-And-A-Long-Term-Binding-To-Unify-Free-Competitive-or-Cooperative-Forces:*
    - By using the comcomized structuring, each of both forces - the competitive (which when comcomized are with less chances for betrayal) or the cooperative (which when comcomized are with less chances of deceiving representative) , are able to be unified not only for terms longer than the usual since the structure is of a company, but also for better managing of their own individual risks, simply since the structure in itself reduces dependency upon those who are too large to fall or are able to be (tempted to be) captured (or bought) for gaining by others control over it;
    - when the positions of "talkers" are ranked equally, the position of the talker cannot any longer qualify her/his arguments (in contrast to qualification by the position of a high ranked spammer and liar talker);
    - centralization is beneficial only for short and well defined terms, whereas decentralized bodies are more balanced lasting longer and are more common in nature.
- *D) It Is Scalable-Organic-Authentic-Dynamic making it a bridge to achieve your gaols*
    - Why? Test what can happen after the success of the personal and the common interest, as they must meet, for scalability to take place in growing social bodies.

Figure-2:The comcomized geek vs the geeknet inc hand of the open source:

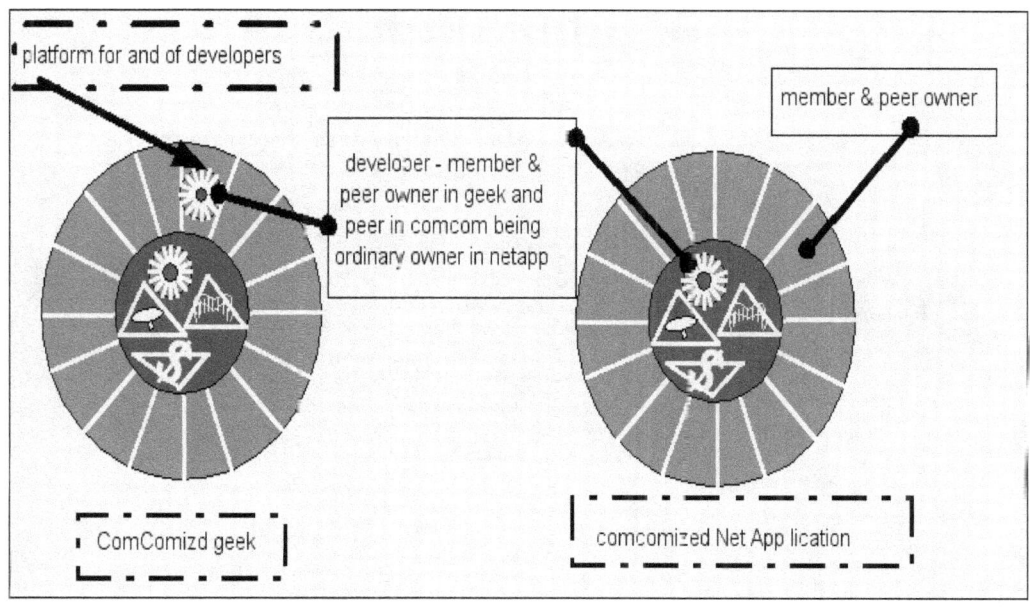

Figure-2-b: the comcomizm ltd can force its polices by forming partnership :

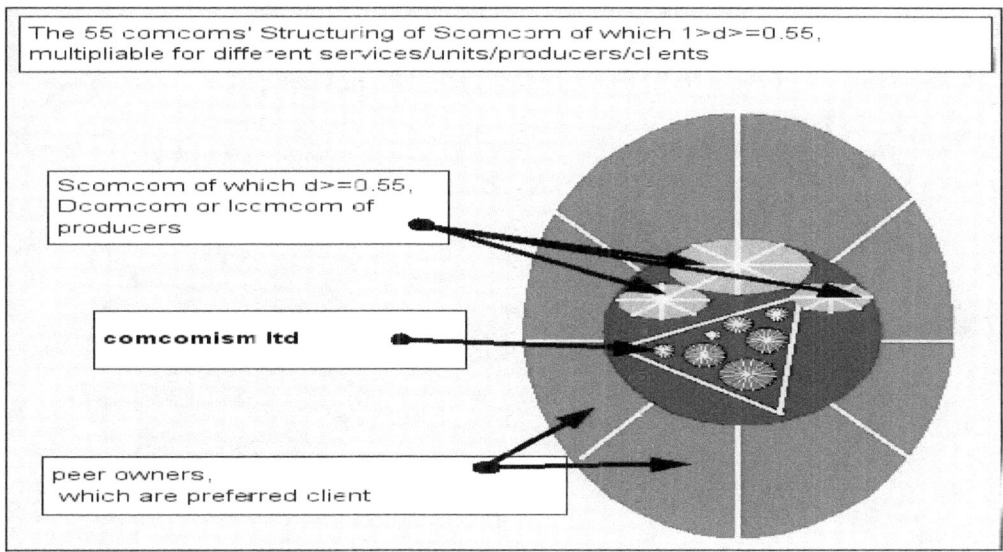

Figure-3: a flayer calling for workshop for comcomsim level A:

Worksop for ComComIsm

It is about realizing equality in this commercialized world and it is a way to get organized by the means of this world (only now) as free and equal owners of the organization.

A 2 hours meeting for learning how to get organized in a comcomized unit, which is a unit of free and equal owners (peer owners, as shareholders having equal number of shares) and is based on a personal agreement of 17 points.

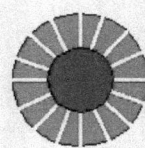

The positions in the outer (red) circle are of owners having equal share, unlike those in the inner (blue) circle. The proportion between both circles is either fixed in Scomcom or changeable in Icomcom or Dcomcom. The number of the peer owners must be agreed by them. Each owner shall directly, or indirectly, obtain no more than one position per a comcomized unit and except for the Icomcomized units the owner can sell her/his share at any time, but only to who accepts the agreement. The price in each such transaction reflects the value of the unit as a whole. Here you can see 2 comcomized units: the one on the left has d =0.50 and on the right has d=1.00.

For more google the term
comcomism
and from the left menu
go @A@ for the agreement
go @W@ for the registration to the workshop
also try http://is-with.wikidot.com/contact

hot		
@A@	@O@	@M@
@W@	@I@	@C@
@DO	@IS	@OM
@GO	@SB	@CS

Figure-4: the comcomized unit can be unites and develop up to down and/or down to up:
On line and *on the ground ,centralized* (up to down) and/or *decriminalized (down to up)* the comcomized communities are now *Growing:*

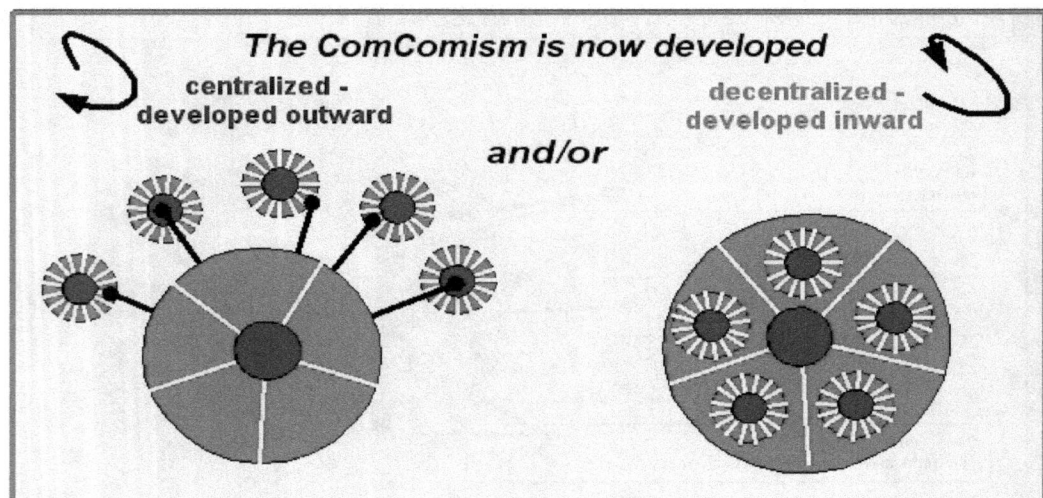

figure-5: the Scomcom of a cause and the apparatus of distribution which can be comcomized.

The Scomcom of the cause:

The d (- the proportion between red and blue) of the SComCom of the cause is fixed for separating between the power of the activists as peer owners (in red) versus the power of the contributers (in blue), so that regardless any amount of contribution, such as by donation, the independence of the activists is kept unchangeable.

(in blue) The contributers for the cause are peer owners of another comcom being ordinary owner of the SComCom of the cause.

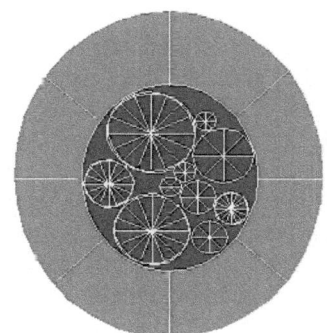

(in red) The activists of the cause are the peer owners in the SComCom of the cause.

The apparatus for distribution of energy

The distribution of the energy here is in return to money, as it's produced by power producers such as artists, developers and/or researchers and as its receptors are preferred clients (in red) above its distributor, such as publish house/s, (in blue) and the artists as the power producers are in the bottom (in green).

...such apparatus when is comcomized is more authentic and effective, as the artists in green are peer owners in Scomcom of which d=1, which is an ordinary owner partnering with the publish house/s (in blue) in another Scomcom of which peer owners (in red) are reworded clients.

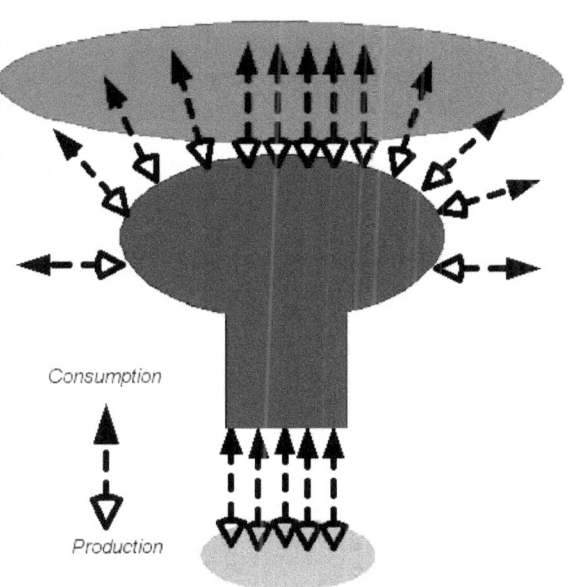

Consumption

Production

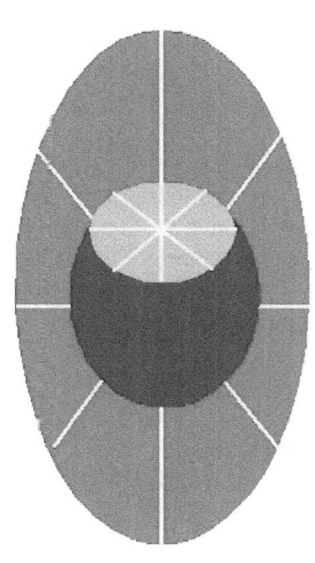

The power producers as competitors, and per any competition (as it is established by the distributors), still have common interest, at least in keeping the condition of (the game allowing) the competition and in improving marketing of their products as the clients might become peer owners in the comcomized apparatus.

The world is now changing! *Are you going to **define** these changes? A proposal:*
Yes, when your democratic organization's ***assets*** are owned equally by all its members***!***
Download the manual for "peer owners" at http://is-with.wikidot.com

Here is a new approach named "Peer Owners": In different groups, people can create and own the changes they want, by increasing the power of each individual in any democratic organization, such that all the assets of the organization are owned equally by all its members (making the organization's membership be ***tradable***)!

Why? This is for never letting takeover by a sole (and bigger) entity and for long lasting realizing the original cause of the organization, while making the people's commercial power be bind with their political one in realizing their own cause. Activists using this way can act "positive" for pulling the "center" to their side. At least one positive statement is always able to be bridged to any negative one.

Here is an example (for bridging to "normal" center, we can be ALSO positive not only anti nuclear energy): In different groups, the people of the city, could and should become peer (equal) owners of solar/wind-power-farms - This creates new market for manufacturing wind-turbines/ solar-panels, and since many "small" owners are to be concern, also some more massive pro green energy demonstration for reducing the green costs, by e.g. bettering the connection to the grid etc.

Likewise, people can also be peer owners of their **bank (**by moving their deposits**)**, **newsagent (**by reading the news from the agencies they own**)**, **isp** (using the Internet Service Provider they own), **publisher** etc. Apropo publisher, are you an *artist*? Me too. Yes, we are *competitors*, but shouldn't we be the ones who *set the rules for such competition*? This is true also for *developers*, *researchers* and *small businesses* etc.

GovComCom (http://fwd4.me/05Su): For breaking the infinite cycle of privatization going to/from nationalization/bailout, list the people in the concern for the excuse of the government to make these people peer owners in the "supported" institutes.

Want to know more?
Search key words: *peer owners*
site:
http://fb.me/peer.owners
This pdf: http://fwd4.me/05Sq
daily online meeting: 20:00-21:00
chat: irc://freenode/peer.owners
Workshop: http://fwd4.me/01y0
Booklet/Manual: http://fwd4.me/zeH
Organizations: http://fwd4.me/01lz
print flyers: http://fwd4.me/zyE
contact : http://fwd4.me/zdw
Search also:: *real democracy*
in Berlin: http://fwd4.me/05LG

https://fb.me/peer.owners

Thanks... ***Providing endless accumulation of power is a root of evil!***

In 6 points - **Peer owners** holding a "**ComCom**"(- standing for **Common Company)**:
1. Based on a contract, any ComComized unit, being one of the 3: Scomcomized, Icomcomized or Dcomcomized, guarantees equality between its peer members being its owners, sitting at its top and owning equal share of it - like shareholders having equal number of its shares.
2. Added together, all the peers own one portion of the unit, as the rest of the unit (if any) is owned by ordinary (non-peer) owners and the ratio of the peers' portion is 'd' (as 'd' times 100 is the percentage), where 'd of Scomcomized unit is only once defined.
3. Each peer owner is either a person or a ComComized unit, where each ordinary owner of Scomcom is either a person or a legal body.
4. Directly or indirectly, holding more than one position in it is forbidden.
5. The number of peers holding it must be agreed independently amongst themselves.
6. Buyers of its shares must agree with all the points establishing ComComized unit.
  The full guidance for the agreements used for comcomizing units: http://fwd4.me/01kT

For organizers on http://fwd4.me/01lz
We are gathering many organizations, each (is to) answer these 4 questions:
A) The contact of at least one of the representatives of organization.
B) In what type of comcom the organization is organized
C) The number of its peer owners which already singed the comcomized contract?
D) The estimated value of the comcom per each year (say from 1 to next 10 years).
With these parameters, we (are to) go to programmers to implement our specification (http://fwd4.me/05Sv) and to investors.

A 2 hours workshop: *http://fwd4.me/01xh*
Name: Becoming Peer Owners.
Where and When: Available http://fwd4.me/zvS or Request http://fwd4.me/01xh
In plan: The first 1/2 hour is mandatory as the rest is optional, of which one or more options can be your issues.
1) +- 1/2 hour: In 6 points, the basic for establishing the agreement between peer owners.
2) +- 1/2 hour: Using the agreement in the agreement of the association and then the association to own the assets/properties of "normal" company, as the assets are licensed to use in specific conditions, like appointing the desired employees.
3) +- 1/2 hour: About the intergeneration of commercial and political power of the people being many, "small" and peer owners, while caring for their own individual interest. e.g. Direction of use - Bettering social and environmental issues; Concrete use: Turning "negative statements of activists" to "positive issues" for the "commercialized" center.
4) +- 1/2 hour : Conceptual and Operational issues. Such as: Why nuclear energy is the most expansive, danger and dirty, in some "well sound" arguments for the "center"; The decentralization of the comcomizing project, including my own goal and commitment.

  For implementing all from mailing list services to stock market of units owned by peers.
Spread (print/send) this http://fwd4.me/05Sq , so that you could find your possible workshop's participants, your partners as peer owners and/or if you are an organizer register your organization for defining this new market for programmers and investors.

You are the owners and leaders - **produce better than me** and license your products.

For reducing falsifying the ComComIsm's objectives, we must be decentralized and diverse. Hence when providing one or more "global centers", such as the "comcomism LTD" it should be held by comcomS, of which *"the d=1"* and of which the peer owners are *comcomism activists* in groups of 10 to 200 (the max of 200 is for keeping familiarity in the groups) http://tinyurl.com/2untb9t .

The comcomism establishes a direct relation of ownership between assets and people - making it suitable for operating any state-recognized organization, such that the organization has no assets, but instead a license to operate over the assets individually owned by the comcom's members collectivity granting the license and authorizing the source of all its appointments. Per each state, the comcomism ltd is to initiate some of such organizations by taking the position of the comcom's members until such members will join in. More http://tinyurl.com/2uqt6pf#post-1010675 .

Our default licensing in this phase is the Attribution-NonCommercial-ShareAlike. We encourage you to hold your ownership over the "things" you produce and/or serve for later on contribute your properties, by using (optionally) other (commercial) licensing of your preference, when looking for your peers and cooperating in comcomS of your preference.

ComComIsm for activist – (when are doing some of these activities):
- *Books and any-other-content* - creating materials such as this book, which is meant to be one of many comcom's product , while keeping it cheap for the buyer and letting free promotional (http://is-with.wikidot.com).
- *Workshops:* (on the ground), so that people could meet the people of their kind, http://tinyurl.com/y97lxbz workshops of 4 levels:
  - "get know it" of 2 hours meeting
  - "get understand it": how to realize it in my life to solve my specific problems.
  - "get use it": how to solve problem raised after initiating comcom
  - "get it trained" for becoming a "recognized"coacher per each of the 4 levels.
- *Authorization and registration*:
  - "identity proof" of 5 elements: first and last names, who invite, recognized authority issuing document of identity and photo able to be identified as the one of the one from the document of identity.
  - Having such "identity proof" of an holder been registered, requires that the holder already agreed to lose all holding registered in the system and in the systems collaborating with it, as it is found that per each such registered ComCom, the holder holds directly, or indirectly, more than one position..
  - Hence the more valuable comcomS are registered in it the stronger is the proof the system can provide. (it might be useful to require reinforcement of the identity every 3 months).
- *Internet (on pc and handy)*:
  - provider for services of mailing lists owned by their members , (as base for farther steps, such "comcom social" a comcomized social networking)
    - http://tinyurl.com/yzu72yy comcomized mailing services ,
    - but at least optionally with security in collaboration on http://fwd4.me/05Sv
  - Holders meeting being supreme over board of directors + E-democracy: including direct democracy or liquid (with delegable proxy) democracy.
  - Marketing of shares: a stock market for shares of peer or ordinary owners, for more see the 55 structure here http://tinyurl.com/2vlecwb

Some tips for your issues: *1)* Demand adding or add the privilege of peer ownership to any membership; *2)* Prefer or provide your best allies with (peer) ownership over licensing or temporal contracts. *3)* Stop central banks feeding banks and other big cooperations in cycles of privatizations and bailouts by demanding GovComComizing such forms, more: http://tinyurl.com/pnx8cx .